Rochester, New York Travel Guide

Hidden Gems, Must-Do Activities, Day Trips,
Maps & Pictures for Exploration

Steven Harper

Map of Rochester

1. Open your device's camera app.
2. Point the camera at the QR code.
3. Ensure the QR code is within the frame and well-lit.
4. Wait for the scanner to recognize and read the code.
5. Tap on the notification or follow the prompt to open the link.
6. Allow access to your location if prompted.
7. View and interact with the map on Google Maps.

About the Author

Steven Harper is a seasoned traveler with an insatiable curiosity for uncovering hidden gems around the world. Born with wanderlust in his veins, Steven has traversed six continents, from the bustling streets of Tokyo to the serene beaches of Bali, and from the rugged landscapes of Patagonia to the historic charm of European villages.

Despite having explored some of the most exotic locations on Earth, Steven found his heart captured by the vibrant city of Rochester, New York. After stumbling upon this upstate treasure during a cross-country road trip, Steven decided to make Rochester his home base between global adventures.

Combining a keen eye for detail honed through years of travel with a deep appreciation for Rochester's unique charm, Steven brings a fresh perspective to the city's travel scene. This guide is the result of countless hours spent exploring Rochester's nooks and crannies, chatting with locals, and experiencing the city's attractions firsthand.

When not writing or exploring, you can find Steven sipping locally roasted coffee at cozy cafes.

Through this guide, Steven hopes to share his passion for Rochester, inspiring both visitors and locals to see the Flower City through the eyes of a world traveler who chose to put down roots in this remarkable corner of New York.

About the Book

Hey there, fellow traveler!

So you're thinking about exploring Rochester, huh? Well, you've just stumbled upon your new best friend. This isn't your average, run-of-the-mill travel guide – oh no. This is your ticket to experiencing Rochester like a true insider, whether you're a first-time visitor or a longtime local looking to rediscover your city.

What's Inside?

Buckle up, because I'm about to take you on a journey through the Flower City that'll make your head spin (in a good way, I promise!).

A Trip Down Memory Lane

I'll kick things off with a stroll through Rochester's fascinating history. Trust me, it's not the boring stuff you dozed through in high school. I'm talking about the juicy bits that'll make you the most interesting person at any cocktail party.

Planning Made Easy

Next up, I've got your back with a foolproof planning section. I broke down everything you need to know to make your Rochester adventure smooth sailing. No more stressing about the details – I've got you covered!

Timing is Everything

Ever shown up somewhere only to find out you just missed the coolest festival of the year? Not on my watch! I'll give you the inside scoop on the best times to visit Rochester, whether you're chasing cherry blossoms or fall foliage.

Pack Like a Pro

Forget about overpacking or forgetting essentials. This packing guide will ensure you're prepared for everything from sunny park days to snowy adventures.

Getting Around Town

I'll show you how to navigate Rochester like a local. And here's the kicker – I've included an interactive map with QR codes. Just scan and go! It's like having a local guide right in your pocket.

Rest Your Head

From luxurious hotels to budget-friendly, I've got the lowdown on the best places to catch some Z's. Sweet dreams are made of these!

Foodie Paradise

Get ready to loosen your belt! I'll introduce you to Rochester's mouthwatering culinary scene. From famous garbage plates to hidden gem cafes, your taste buds are in for a treat.

Itineraries for Every Traveler

Whether you're here for a weekend or a week, traveling solo or with a gaggle of kids, I've crafted itineraries to make every moment count.

Bonus: Your Personal Rochester Journal

Here's where things get really special. I've included a reflective journal section for you to jot down your thoughts, favorite moments, and maybe even paste in a few ticket stubs. Years from now, you'll open this guide and be transported right back to your Rochester adventure.

But wait, there's more! (Always wanted to say that.) I've packed this guide with local tips, hidden gems, and day trip ideas that'll make you feel like you've unlocked secret levels of Rochester.

So, are you ready to dive in? Rochester is waiting for you, and trust me, it's got some surprises up its sleeve. Let's go explore!

Copyright

Contents

"To travel is to live." –
Hans Christian Andersen

Introduction

I'll admit it: when I first told my friends I was planning a trip to Rochester, NY, they looked at me as if I'd announced I was moving to the moon. "Rochester?" they echoed, brows furrowed in confusion. "Isn't that just... cold?"

Oh, how little they knew. And to be honest, how little I knew too. But I had a hunch about this city situated along the southern shore of Lake Ontario, a whisper of promise that urged me to book that ticket and pack my bags. Spoiler alert: that hunch was right on the money.

As my plane descended through the clouds, the first thing that struck me was the patchwork of green below, interspersed with the glint of sunlight on water. This wasn't the industrial landscape I'd half-expected. This was... beautiful.

My adventure began the moment I set foot in the city. There's something in the air in Rochester – a palpable energy, a sense of both history and innovation intertwining. I felt it as I strolled down East Avenue, admiring the blend of stately mansions and modern buildings, each with a story to tell.

My first stop was the Strong National Museum of Play. Now, I consider myself a mature, sophisticated traveler, but let me tell you, I giggled like a schoolkid as I explored the interactive exhibits. From vintage arcade games to the world's largest collection of dolls, this place is a treasure trove of nostalgia and fun. I even found myself in a heated game of giant Tetris with a seven-year-old (she won, but I maintain it was beginner's luck).

All that "playing" worked up quite an appetite, which led me to a Rochester culinary institution: the infamous "Garbage Plate." Don't let the name fool you – this delicious mess of potatoes, mac salad, meat, and a special sauce is a flavor explosion that should be on every foodie's bucket list. As I savored each bite, I couldn't help but chuckle at the irony of finding gourmet bliss in something called "garbage."

With a full belly and a child-like grin, I made my way to the George Eastman Museum. As a photography enthusiast, I was in heaven. The sprawling mansion, once home to the founder of Kodak, now houses an incredible collection of photographs and film artifacts. I left feeling inspired and itching to capture some Rochester moments of my own.

As the sun began to set, I found myself drawn to the gentle roar of High Falls. The sight of this 96-foot waterfall in the heart of the city took my breath away. I stood there, mesmerized by the golden light dancing on the cascading water, and felt a profound sense of peace. Here, in the midst of a vibrant city, was this natural wonder – a perfect metaphor for Rochester itself, I thought.

Throughout my stay, I was continuously charmed by the friendly locals, always ready with a smile and a recommendation for their favorite hidden gem. There's a warmth to Rochesterians that belies the city's chilly reputation.

From the world-class museums to the quirky local festivals (Lilac Festival, anyone?), from the rich history to the exciting food scene, Rochester packed more surprises into a few days than I'd found in weeks of traveling elsewhere. It's a city that seamlessly blends urban sophistication with small-town charm, innovation with tradition, and natural beauty with urban landscapes.

As I reluctantly boarded my flight home, already planning my return trip, I couldn't help but smile at how wrong my friends had been. Cold? Maybe sometimes. But Rochester, NY is anything but cold in spirit. It's a warm, vibrant, endlessly fascinating destination that deserves a top spot on any traveler's wish list.

So, why visit Rochester, NY? Because it's a city that will surprise you, charm you, and leave you wondering why you didn't visit sooner. Pack your sense of adventure (and maybe your stretchy pants for that Garbage Plate), and prepare to fall in love with this hidden gem of a city. Rochester is waiting to delight you, just as it delighted me. Who knows? You might just discover your new favorite destination in a place you never expected.

Why Visit Rochester NY?

Situated along the southern shore of Lake Ontario, Rochester, NY is a city that often flies under the radar of many travelers. But don't let its low profile fool you – this gem of a city has a treasure trove of experiences waiting for those who venture here. As someone who's fallen head over heels for Rochester's charm, let me tell you: this place is special.

You might be wondering, "What's so great about Rochester?" Well, grab a cup of coffee (or better yet, a local Genesee beer), and let me count the ways. Here's why Rochester should be your next travel destination:

1. **A Feast for Your Taste Buds**: Foodies, rejoice! Rochester's culinary scene is a delightful mix of comfort food and innovative cuisine. You can't leave without trying the infamous "Garbage Plate" – trust me, it's way more delicious than it sounds. And don't get me started on the Rochester-style pizza or the mouthwatering beef on weck sandwiches.

2. **Four Seasons of Fun**: Whether you're a sun-seeker or a snow bunny, Rochester's got you covered. Summers are perfect for exploring the city's many parks and festivals, while winters transform the landscape into a wonderland of skiing, ice skating, and cozy fireside chats.

3. **A Cultural Powerhouse**: For a mid-sized city, Rochester punches way above its weight in culture. The Eastman School of Music attracts world-class talent, while the Rochester Philharmonic Orchestra will

serenade your soul. Art lovers can lose themselves in the Memorial Art Gallery, home to works spanning 5000 years of human creativity.

4. **Family-Friendly Adventures**: Got kids? They'll love you forever if you take them to The Strong National Museum of Play. It's not just any museum – it's an interactive wonderland dedicated to the history and exploration of play. Even as an adult, I couldn't resist the urge to join in!

5. **Natural Beauty Galore**: Mother Nature really outdid herself here. From the stunning High Falls right in the heart of downtown to the nearby Finger Lakes region, you're never far from breathtaking scenery. Letchworth State Park, often called the "Grand Canyon of the East," is just a short drive away.

6. **A History Buff's Dream**: Rochester played a pivotal role in American history, particularly in the women's rights and abolitionist movements. The Susan B. Anthony House and Frederick Douglass sites offer powerful glimpses into the past.

7. **Festival City**: Rochesterians know how to party. The Lilac Festival in May is a blooming celebration of spring, while the

Rochester International Jazz Festival in June attracts music lovers from around the globe.

8. **Affordable Adventures**: Your wallet will thank you. Rochester offers big-city amenities at small-town prices, making it an ideal destination for budget-conscious travelers who don't want to skimp on experiences.

9. **Innovation Hub**: From its days as the birthplace of Kodak and Xerox to its current status as a hotbed for optics and photonics research, Rochester has always been at the forefront of innovation. The city's energy is infectious – you can feel the buzz of creativity in the air.

10. **Genuine Hospitality**: Last but certainly not least, the people of Rochester are some of the friendliest you'll ever meet. Don't be surprised if you start a conversation with a stranger and end up with dinner recommendations, travel tips, and maybe even an invitation to a backyard BBQ.

So there you have it – a whirlwind tour of why Rochester, NY should be on your travel radar. It's a city that surprises, delights, and leaves you wondering why you didn't visit sooner. Pack your bags (and your sense of adventure) and get ready to fall in love with Rochester. Who knows? Like me, you might just find yourself planning your next visit before you've even left.

Chapter One: Understanding Rochester NY

Geography and Climate

Rochester, New York, is a city that wears its geography on its sleeve and its climate like a badge of honor. Nestled along the southern shore of Lake Ontario, this vibrant urban center is a testament to the beauty and diversity of upstate New York's landscape.

Geographically speaking, Rochester is a city of water. The mighty Genesee River cuts through its heart, creating the dramatic High Falls right in the downtown area. This isn't just pretty – it's history carved in stone, a reminder of the river's role in powering the city's early industries. The river's path through Rochester creates a unique topography, with ridges and valleys adding character to the cityscape.

But it's not all urban jungle. Rochester is nicknamed the "Flower City" for good reason. It's home to Highland Park, a horticultural wonderland designed by Frederick Law Olmsted (the same guy who designed Central Park in NYC). The park explodes into a riot of color each spring during the famous Lilac Festival.

Just a stone's throw from the city, you'll find yourself in the stunning Finger Lakes region. These long, narrow lakes, carved by glaciers eons ago, offer a playground for nature lovers and wine enthusiasts alike. It's like Mother Nature decided to place an adventure park right in Rochester's backyard.

Now, let's talk weather. Rochester experiences a humid continental climate, which is a fancy way of saying "we get a bit of everything." Summers are warm and pleasant, with temperatures typically ranging from the mid-60s to low 80s Fahrenheit.

It's perfect for outdoor festivals, lakeside picnics, or just lounging in one of the city's many parks.

Winter, on the other hand, is when Rochester really shows its true colors – mostly white. The city gets an average of about 100 inches of snow annually, thanks to its position in the Great Lakes snow belt. While this might sound daunting, Rochesterians have turned winter into an art form. Skiing, ice skating, and building impressively elaborate snowmen are practically civic duties here.

Spring and fall are transitions of beauty in Rochester. Spring brings a burst of color as the city's many gardens and parks come to life. Fall paints the landscape in warm hues, making it a perfect time for scenic drives or hikes in nearby parks.

One thing to note: Rochester's weather can be a bit... unpredictable. It's not uncommon to experience all four seasons in a single week (sometimes even in a single day!). Locals often joke that if you don't like the weather, just wait five minutes. This variability keeps things interesting and is part of Rochester's charm.

Despite (or perhaps because of) its climatic mood swings, Rochester's geography and weather help shape its character. They've fostered a community that's resilient, adaptable, and always ready to make the most of whatever Mother Nature throws their way. Whether you're basking in the summer sun by the lake or sledding down snowy hills, Rochester's geography and climate ensure there's never a dull moment.

A Brief History of Rochester

Alright, buckle up for a whirlwind tour through Rochester's past! This city's story is as colorful and varied as a bag of Wegmans' salt potatoes (trust me, you'll want to try those when you visit).

Let's kick things off in the late 18th century. The area we now call Rochester was originally home to the Seneca people, part of the Iroquois Confederacy. They called this place "the land of milk and honey" – clearly, they were onto something good.

Fast forward to 1803, and enter our founding father figure: one Colonel Nathaniel Rochester. This guy bought a 100-acre tract along the Genesee River, probably thinking, "Hey, this looks like a nice spot for a city!" Spoiler alert: he was right.

By 1817, the settlement was incorporated as Rochesterville (bit of a mouthful, if you ask me). Just a few years later, in 1823, they ditched the "ville" and became plain old Rochester. I guess they realized shorter names are easier to fit on t-shirts.

Now, here's where things get interesting. Rochester hit the jackpot with the Erie Canal. When it opened in 1825, it turned the city into a boomtown practically overnight. Suddenly, Rochester was the place to be if you were in the flour milling business. They didn't call it the "Flour City" for nothing!

But Rochester wasn't content with just one nickname. As the flour industry waned, the city bloomed into the "Flower City," thanks to its thriving nursery businesses. Talk about a glow-up, right?

The 19th century was when Rochester really flexed its muscles. It became a hotbed of social reform movements. Susan B. Anthony called Rochester home as she fought for women's rights. Frederick Douglass published his abolitionist newspaper, "The North Star," right here. These folks weren't just talking about change – they were making it happen.

Then came the big names that put Rochester on the global map. George Eastman founded Kodak here in 1888, forever changing the world of photography. Xerox followed in 1906, because apparently, Rochester had a thing for imaging companies.

The 20th century brought its own ups and downs. Rochester rode the waves of industrial boom and bust, always finding ways to reinvent itself. When traditional manufacturing declined, the city leaned into education and technology. The University of Rochester and Rochester Institute of Technology became powerhouses, churning out innovations and smart cookies by the dozen.

Today's Rochester is a city that honors its past while looking firmly to the future. It's a place where you can grab a plate of dinosaur-shaped chicken nuggets at the National Museum of Play, then head over to a cutting-edge optics lab. It's a city that's seen its share of challenges but always comes back stronger, armed with a "we've got this" attitude and probably a Garbage Plate or two.

So there you have it – Rochester's history in a nutshell. From flour mills to flower fields, from social reformers to tech innovators, this city's story is one of constant evolution. And the best part? The next chapter is still being written. Who knows? Your visit might just become a part of Rochester's ongoing history.

"Travel makes one modest. You see what a tiny place you occupy in the world." – Gustave Flaubert

Chapter Two: Planning Your Rochester Adventure

Best times to visit Rochester NY

L et's talk timing. When's the best time to pack your bags and head to Rochester? Well, the short answer is: it depends on what you're after. But don't worry, I've got you covered for every season.

Let's kick off with summer, shall we? June through August is when Rochester really shines. The weather's warm (think highs in the 70s and 80s Fahrenheit), and the city comes alive with festivals and outdoor events. The Corn Hill Arts Festival in July is a personal favorite – imagine streets lined with art, the smell of food in the air, and live music at every corner. It's like the whole city turns into one big block party!

But here's a pro tip: if you're not a fan of crowds, maybe skip the last week of July. That's when the Rochester Jazz Festival happens, and while it's amazing, the city gets packed. Hotel prices shoot up faster than a teenager's hand at a free pizza giveaway.

Now, fall in Rochester? That's something special. September and October bring crisp air and a explosion of colors that'll make your Instagram followers green with envy. It's perfect for hiking in nearby parks or taking a drive through the Finger Lakes region. Plus, you can hit up local farms for apple picking and hayrides. Nothing says "fall" like sipping fresh apple cider while pretending you're not lost in a corn maze.

Winter in Rochester is... an experience. If you're into snow sports, you'll be in heaven from December through February. The city gets blanketed in white, and nearby Bristol Mountain becomes a playground for skiers and snowboarders. Just pack your warmest coat – it can get pretty nippy out there!

But here's where it gets interesting: Rochester doesn't hibernate in winter. The Lamberton Conservatory in Highland Park becomes a tropical oasis in the middle of a snow globe. And don't even get me started on the hot chocolate scene – it's seriously next level.

Spring is Rochester's comeback season. April and May see the city shaking off its winter coat and bursting into bloom. The annual Lilac Festival in May is a riot of color and fragrance. Fair warning though: spring weather in Rochester can be as unpredictable as a cat's mood. One day it's t-shirt weather, the next you're digging out your winter boots again. But hey, that's part of the charm!

Here's a little secret: personally, I'm a big fan of visiting in early June or late September. You get great weather without the peak season crowds and prices. Plus, there's something magical about those long, warm evenings when the whole city seems to be out enjoying patios and parks.

Remember, no matter when you visit, Rochester's got something up its sleeve. This city knows how to make the most of every season. So whether you're building snowmen in February or sipping craft beer on a sunny patio in July, you're in for a good time. Just don't forget to pack a variety of clothes – Rochester likes to keep you on your toes!

What to Pack

Let's talk packing for Rochester. First things first: forget about packing light. This city's weather is as changeable as a chameleon on a disco floor, so you'll want to be prepared for anything.

Let's start with the basics. No matter when you're visiting, throw in some layers. A light jacket or sweater is a must, even in summer. Rochester evenings can get chilly faster than you can say "Garbage Plate."

Speaking of Garbage Plates, pack your stretchiest pants. Rochester's food scene is no joke, and you'll want to be comfortable as you eat your way through the city.

Now, if you're coming in winter, channel your inner Eskimo. A warm coat, hat, gloves, and boots are non-negotiable. Snow is practically Rochester's unofficial mascot from December to March. And don't forget your thermals – they'll be your best friends when you're exploring outdoor winter attractions like the ice rink at Martin Luther King Jr. Memorial Park.

Summer visitors, don't get too cocky. While you can leave the parka at home, do pack a rain jacket and umbrella. Rochester summers can bring sudden showers that pop up faster than a prairie dog. Oh, and sunscreen! Just because you're not in Florida doesn't mean the sun isn't working overtime.

If you're planning on exploring the great outdoors (and you should – the Finger Lakes region is gorgeous), comfortable walking shoes are a must. Your feet will thank you after a day of hiking in Letchworth State Park or strolling through the Rochester Public Market.

Here's a pro tip: pack a backpack or day bag. It's perfect for carrying around that extra layer, your water bottle (staying hydrated is key when you're sampling all those local craft beers), and any souvenirs you pick up along the way.

Don't forget your camera! Rochester is full of Instagram-worthy spots, from the High Falls to the colorful street art downtown. If you're old school, pack a journal too. You'll want to remember all the quirky details of your Rochester adventure.

Last but not least, bring your sense of adventure and an open mind. Rochester is full of surprises, and the best experiences often come when you least expect them. Who knows? You might find yourself trying on a Wegmans shirt and wearing it unironically by the end of your trip.

You can always pick up anything you've forgotten at one of Rochester's many shops. So don't stress too much about packing. As long as you're prepared for a bit of everything, you'll be ready to tackle whatever Rochester throws your way. Now get packing, and get ready for an unforgettable trip!

Rochester Travel Essentials

Alright, future Rochester explorer, let's get you prepped with some essential info. Think of this as your cheat sheet for navigating the Flower City like a pro.

First up, getting here. If you're flying in, you'll land at the Frederick Douglass - Greater Rochester International Airport. It's a mouthful, I know, but locals just call it ROC. It's small but mighty, just 10 minutes from downtown. No need for a sherpa to guide you through this airport!

Now, about getting around. Rochester's got a decent public bus system called RTS. It'll get you to most places, but honestly, it's not always the most convenient. If you're staying downtown, your own two feet can take you pretty far. But if you want to explore beyond the city center (and trust me, you do), renting a car is your best bet. Just remember, parallel parking is considered an Olympic sport here.

Speaking of downtown, that's where you'll find most hotels. But don't overlook neighborhoods like the East End or South Wedge. They're full of character and great Airbnb options. Plus, you'll feel like a local in no time.

Let's talk money. Rochester is pretty wallet-friendly compared to bigger cities. A decent meal will set you back about $15-20, and a local beer is around $5-7. Most attractions are reasonably priced too. The Strong Museum of Play, for example, is $18 for adults. Not bad for a day of nostalgia-fueled fun!

Now, a word about the weather. Rochester likes to keep you on your toes. It can be sunny one minute and raining the next. In winter, snow is less of a weather condition and more of a way of life. But don't worry, Rochesterians are snow ninjas. The city rarely shuts down, no matter how much the sky dumps on us.

Here's a local tip: download the WYSL Weather app. It's eerily accurate for Rochester weather. You'll be predicting lake effect snow like a meteorologist in no time.

Oh, and let's not forget about tipping! It's customary to tip 15-20% at restaurants. We're a friendly bunch here, and your servers will appreciate it.

Now, emergency info. The standard 911 works for any emergency. For non-emergencies, Rochester Police can be reached at (585) 428-6720. The biggest hospital is Strong Memorial, but hopefully, your only medical need will be treating a food coma from too many Garbage Plates.

Lastly, embrace the local lingo. If someone tells you to grab a pop, they mean a soda. And if you hear "Wegmans," just know it's not just a grocery store, it's a way of life here.

Rochesterians are a friendly bunch. Don't be afraid to ask for directions or recommendations. We love showing off our city to visitors. Now go out there and explore! Rochester's waiting for you, in all its quirky, charming glory.

Rochester Year-Round Festival

Festival lovers, listen up! Rochester's got a party for every season, and trust me, these folks know how to celebrate.

Kick off the year with the Lakeside Winter Celebration in February. Yeah, it's cold, but hot chocolate and ice sculptures make it worth it.

Come May, the city explodes in purple for the Lilac Festival. It's like Mother Nature's perfume department went wild.

Summer's when things really heat up. The Jazz Festival in June is massive - we're talking nine days of cool cats and hot tunes. July brings the Corn Hill Arts Festival, where you can snag unique crafts and stuff your face with festival food.

Fall? Oh, we've got the KeyBank Rochester Fringe Festival. It's weird, it's wonderful, and it's absolutely unmissable.

And don't think winter slows us down. The Winterfest at Ontario Beach Park in December will have you roasting chestnuts and sipping cider like you're in a holiday movie.

So pack your party pants (make them stretchy - there's a lot of festival food to try) and get ready to festival-hop Rochester style!

Getting To and Around Rochester NY

Getting Here

Alright, let's talk about how to get your feet on Rochester soil. First up, we've got the Frederick Douglass - Greater Rochester International Airport (ROC). Don't let the long name fool you – it's a cozy little airport just a stone's throw (okay, three miles) from downtown. And trust me, your wallet will thank you for flying here.

ROC's got a decent lineup of airlines: Allegiant, American, Delta, Frontier, JetBlue, Southwest, and United. So whether you're a budget traveler or like to fly fancy, we've got you covered.

Not a fan of flying? No worries! New York Trailways has got your back if you're coming from another NY city or even Toronto or Montreal. Their buses are like the cool cousins of school buses – safe, modern, and they won't make you sit next to that kid eating paste.

For the train enthusiasts out there, Amtrak rolls into town daily. It's perfect if you're coming from the Northeast and want to pretend you're in a vintage movie scene.

Getting Around

Once you're here, getting around is easier than explaining what a Garbage Plate is (trust me, you'll find out soon enough).

If you brought your car, congrats! You've just won the jackpot of easy driving. Rochester traffic is about as chill as it gets. Most trips around the city and neighborhoods take about 15-20 minutes. Rush hour here is more like a gentle nudge hour.

No car? No problem! Our Rochester Transit Center on Mortimer St. is like the Grand Central of buses, minus the chaos. For just a buck a ride, you can hop on a bus and explore to your heart's content. The center's got 30 bus bays handling 100 buses an hour – it's like a well-choreographed bus ballet.

The transit center itself is pretty swanky. It's enclosed and climate-controlled, so you won't freeze your buns off in winter or melt into a puddle in summer while waiting for your bus.

But here's a pro tip: if you really want to get the inside scoop on Rochester, hook up with a tour. You can cruise down the Erie Canal (way cooler than it sounds, I promise), sip your way through Finger Lakes wine country, or geek out on some Rochester history.

So there you have it! Whether you're flying, driving, busing, training, or touring, Rochester's ready to welcome you with open arms. Now get moving – there's a Garbage Plate with your name on it waiting somewhere in this wonderful city!

Chapter Three: Where to Stay

Your Home Away from Home

Looking for the perfect place to rest your head in Rochester? You're in luck! This charming city offers a variety of accommodations to suit every taste and budget. Here are some top picks that'll make your stay in the Flower City unforgettable.

1. The Strathallan Rochester Hotel & Spa - A DoubleTree by Hilton

Address: 550 East Ave, Rochester, NY 14607, United States

Phone: +1 585-461-5010

If you're after a touch of luxury, The Strathallan is your go-to. Nestled in the artsy East Avenue neighborhood, this hotel screams sophistication.

Why you'll love it: The rooftop lounge. Trust me, sipping a cocktail while taking in panoramic views of Rochester's skyline is an experience you won't forget.

My take: I stayed here last summer and was blown away by the service. The staff went above and beyond to make me feel at home. The rooms are spacious and modern, and the on-site restaurant, Char, serves up some mean steaks.

The Strathallan Rochester Hotel & Spa - A DoubleTree by Hilton

The Strathallan Rochester Hot...
550 East Ave, Rochester, NY 14607
4.4 ★★★★★ 1,632 reviews
Directions
View larger map

1. Open your device's camera app.
2. Point the camera at the QR code.
3. Ensure the QR code is within the frame and well-lit.
4. Wait for the scanner to recognize and read the code.
5. Tap on the notification or follow the prompt to open the link.
6. Allow access to your location if prompted.
7. View and interact with the map on Google Maps.

2. The Inn on Broadway

Address: 26 Broadway, Rochester, NY 14607, United States

Phone: +1 585-232-3595

Housed in a beautifully restored 1929 building, this boutique hotel oozes charm and character.

Why you'll love it: Location, location, location! You're right in the heart of downtown, perfect for exploring Rochester's attractions on foot.

My take: It's like stepping back in time, but with all the modern amenities you need. The rooms are cozy and unique – no cookie-cutter designs here. Just be warned, the complimentary breakfast is so good, you might need to loosen your belt a notch!

3. Hilton Garden Inn Rochester Downtown

Address: 155 E Main St, Rochester, NY 14604, USA

Phone: +1 585-232-5000

For travelers who appreciate reliability and consistency, this Hilton offers a solid choice right in the city center.

Why you'll love it: The indoor pool is a great way to unwind after a day of sightseeing, especially if you're visiting during Rochester's chilly winters.

My take: While it might not have the unique charm of some boutique hotels, it more than makes up for it in comfort and convenience. I've always found the rooms to be spotless, and the staff is consistently friendly. Plus, being able to earn or use Hilton points is a nice bonus for frequent travelers.

4. The Del Monte Lodge Renaissance Rochester Hotel & Spa

Address: 41 N Main St, Pittsford, NY 14534, USA

Phone: +1 585-381-9900

If you don't mind staying a bit outside the city center, this hotel in the suburb of Pittsford is a real gem.

Why you'll love it: The Erie Canal views are stunning, and the nearby Schoen Place is perfect for a leisurely stroll or grabbing a bite to eat.

My take: This place feels more like a resort than a hotel. The spa is top-notch – treat yourself to a massage, you won't regret it. It's a bit pricier than some other options, but the peaceful setting and luxurious amenities make it worth the splurge.

5. School 31 Lofts

Address: 208 N Goodman St, Rochester, NY 14607, USA

Phone: +1 585-510-1100

For something completely different, why not stay in a converted school building? These apartment-style accommodations offer a unique experience.

Why you'll love it: The novelty factor is off the charts. How often do you get to say you slept in a classroom?

My take: I was skeptical at first, but ended up loving my stay here. The lofts are spacious and well-equipped, perfect if you're planning a longer visit or traveling with family. The historic touches, like original chalkboards in some units, add a fun, quirky vibe.

Rochester has something for everyone. Whether you're here for business, pleasure, or a bit of both, you're sure to find a hotel that feels just right. Happy travels!

1. **Open your device's camera app.**
2. **Point the camera at the QR code.**
3. **Ensure the QR code is within the frame and well-lit.**
4. **Wait for the scanner to recognize and read the code.**
5. **Tap on the notification or follow the prompt to open the link.**
6. **Allow access to your location if prompted.**
7. **View and interact with the map on Google Maps.**

"The world is a book, and those who do not travel read only one page." – Saint Augustine

Chapter Four: What to Eat?

Hey there, fellow food lovers! Buckle up (and maybe loosen that belt a notch) because I've about to take your taste buds on a wild ride through Rochester's culinary scene. From iconic local dishes to farm-fresh delights, Rochester's got a little something for everyone. So grab a napkin — things might get messy!

1. The Legendary Garbage Plate

Let's kick things off with Rochester's claim to fame: the Garbage Plate. Don't let the name fool you — this messy mountain of deliciousness is a local treasure. Picture this: a base of home fries and macaroni salad, topped with your choice of burger patties, hot dogs, or sausage, then smothered in a spicy meat sauce, onions, and mustard. It's a heart-stopping, hunger-busting feast that's perfect after a night out (or, let's be honest, any time).

Where to get it: Nick Tahou Hots is the originator, but locals swear by dogtown for a modern twist on this classic.

2. Rochester's Own White Hot

Move over, regular hot dogs! Rochester's got its own spin on this American classic. The White Hot is a uncured, unsmoked hot dog made from a blend of pork, beef, and veal. It's got a unique flavor that's milder and sweeter than your typical red hot. Throw it on a bun with some mustard and onions, and you're in for a true Rochester experience.

Where to get it: Zweigle's is the brand to look for. Try one at Schaller's Drive-In for the full experience.

3. Abbott's Frozen Custard

Creamy, dreamy, and oh-so-smooth — Abbott's Frozen Custard is the stuff of legends. This isn't your run-of-the-mill ice cream; it's richer, denser, and dare we say, better. On a hot summer day, there's nothing quite like an Abbott's chocolate almond custard cone to cool you down and satisfy your sweet tooth.

Where to get it: Abbott's has several locations around Rochester, but the original shop on Lake Avenue is where the magic began.

4. Zweigles Chicken Chicken

No, that's not a typo. Zweigles Chicken Chicken is a unique Rochester specialty - a chicken sausage packed with, you guessed it, more chicken! It's leaner than your typical sausage but packed with flavor. Grill it up, throw it on a roll, and you've got yourself a taste of Rochester summer.

Where to get it: Pick up a pack at any local grocery store, or try one at Swan Market, a German deli that's been serving Rochester since 1929.

5. Rochester-Style Pizza

Thin crust? Chicago deep dish? Nah, Rochester's got its own pizza style. Think a fluffy, thick crust that's crispy on the bottom, topped with a sweet tomato sauce and plenty of cup-and-char pepperoni. It's a perfect balance of textures and flavors that'll have you reaching for another slice.

Where to get it: Pontillo's and Mark's Pizzeria are local favorites, but don't miss out on the "Pizza Logs" at Salvatore's - they're like pizza egg rolls!

6. Dinosaur Bar-B-Que

Okay, so it's not unique to Rochester (the original is in Syracuse), but Dinosaur Bar-B-Que has become such a staple of the Rochester food scene that we can't leave it out. Their slow-smoked meats and tangy sauces are the stuff barbecue dreams are made of. The pulled pork is a classic, but don't sleep on the brisket.

Where to get it: There's only one location in Rochester, right downtown on Court Street. Get there early on weekends — this place fills up fast!

7. Tom Wahl's Root Beer

Wash down all that amazing food with a frosty mug of Tom Wahl's root beer. This locally made soda has been quenching Rochester's thirst since 1955. It's creamy, it's fizzy, and it's the perfect accompaniment to a burger and fries.

Where to get it: Any Tom Wahl's location. For the full experience, get it in a frosted mug with a scoop of Perry's ice cream for a root beer float.

8. Genesee Cream Ale

If you're in the mood for something a little stronger, reach for a "Genny Cream." This smooth, easy-drinking ale has been a Rochester staple since 1960. It's got a cult following that extends well beyond the city limits.

Where to get it: Any bar in Rochester will have it, but for the full experience, take a tour of the Genesee Brew House and enjoy a cold one with a view of High Falls.

There you have it, food adventurers — a tasty tour through Rochester's must-eat foods. From late-night garbage plates to sweet frozen custard, from unique hot dogs to Rochester-style pizza, this city's got flavors you won't find anywhere else. So come hungry, leave happy, and don't forget to pack your stretchy pants!

"Life is either a daring adventure or nothing at all." – Helen Keller

Chapter Five: Things to do in Rochester NY

Rochester, NY: A Visitor's Guide

Rochester, New York, might not be the first city that comes to mind when planning a trip, but trust me, this hidden gem in western New York has a lot to offer. From its rich history to its vibrant arts scene and natural beauty, Rochester is a city that will surprise and delight you. So, pack your bags and get ready to explore the "Flower City" with this guide to the top things to do in Rochester.

1. Explore the George Eastman Museum

Address: 900 East Ave, Rochester, NY 14607, USA

Hours: Opens 10 am

Opened: 1949

Built: 1905; 119 years ago; 1949; 75 years ago (museum opened)

Architect: J. Foster Warner

Phone: +1 585-327-4800

Architectural styles: Georgian architecture, Colonial Revival architecture

You can't visit Rochester without paying homage to its most famous resident, George Eastman, the founder of Kodak. The George Eastman Museum is housed in his stunning Colonial Revival mansion and is a must-visit for anyone interested in photography, film, or local history.

As you wander through the beautifully preserved rooms, you'll get a glimpse into the life of this innovative entrepreneur. But the real treat is the museum's vast collection of photographs and film artifacts. From early daguerreotypes to modern digital prints, the museum offers a fascinating journey through the history of photography.

Don't miss the Dryden Theatre, where you can catch screenings of classic and contemporary films. If you're lucky, you might even get to hear the restored pipe organ in action – it's quite an experience!

2. Smell the Roses at Highland Park

Address: 180 Reservoir Ave, Rochester, NY 14620, USA

Hours: Opens 10 am

Phone: +1 585-753-7270

If you're visiting Rochester in May, you're in for a treat. The Lilac Festival at Highland Park is one of the city's most beloved events, drawing flower enthusiasts from all over the country. But even if you miss the festival, Highland Park is worth a visit any time of year.

This 150-acre park is home to over 1,200 lilac bushes representing 500 varieties, as well as a stunning array of other flowers and trees. Take a leisurely stroll along the winding paths, have a picnic on the grass, or climb to the top of the Reservoir for panoramic views of the city.

In the winter, the park transforms into a winter wonderland, perfect for sledding or cross-country skiing. It's a reminder that Rochester is beautiful in every season.

3. Step Back in Time at the Strong National Museum of Play

Address: 1 Manhattan Square Dr, Rochester, NY 14607, USA

Hours: Opens 10 am

Founded: 1969

Owner: The Strong

Phone: +1 585-263-2700

Parent organization: The Strong

Who says museums are just for grown-ups? The Strong National Museum of Play is a one-of-a-kind attraction that will bring out the kid in everyone. This massive museum is dedicated to the history and exploration of play, and it's an absolute blast for visitors of all ages.

From the moment you step inside and see the larger-than-life Berenstain Bears treehouse, you know you're in for something special. Explore the World Video Game Hall of Fame, try your hand at classic arcade games, or take a ride on the fully restored 1918 carousel.

One of the highlights is the Toy Halls of Fame, where you can see beloved toys from different eras and even play with some of them. It's a nostalgic trip down memory lane for adults and an exciting adventure for kids.

4. Indulge Your Taste Buds at the Rochester Public Market

Foodies, rejoice! The Rochester Public Market is a feast for the senses and a must-visit destination for anyone who loves good food. This bustling market has been operating since 1905 and is open year-round, rain or shine.

As you wander through the market, you'll find everything from fresh local produce to artisanal cheeses, baked goods, and international specialties. The market is especially lively on Saturdays when it's packed with vendors and shoppers.

Don't leave without trying a "garbage plate" – a Rochester culinary invention that's a hearty mix of meat, potatoes, and macaroni salad. It might not sound elegant, but it's delicious and quintessentially Rochester.

4. Take in the View at High Falls

Address: 4 Commercial St, Rochester, NY 14614, USA

Hours: Open 24 hours

Total height: 96 ft (29 m)

Did you know that Rochester has a 96-foot waterfall right in the heart of downtown? High Falls is a stunning natural wonder that offers a unique urban waterfall experience. The best view is from the Pont de Rennes pedestrian bridge, where you can see the falls in all their glory and get a great view of the city skyline.

For a deeper dive into the area's history, visit the High Falls Interpretive Center and Museum. You'll learn about how the falls powered Rochester's early industries and shaped the city's development.

In the evening, stick around for the illumination of the falls. The colorful light display turns this natural wonder into a mesmerizing nighttime attraction.

5. Catch a Show at Geva Theatre Center

Address: 75 Woodbury Blvd, Rochester, NY 14609, United States

Phone: +1 585-232-4382

Rochester has a thriving arts scene, and at the heart of it is the Geva Theatre Center. This professional theater company puts on a diverse range of

productions throughout the year, from classic plays to cutting-edge contemporary works.

The theater itself is housed in a beautifully renovated historic building that used to be a naval armory. With its intimate setting and excellent acoustics, there's not a bad seat in the house.

Even if you're not a regular theatergoer, catching a show at Geva is a great way to experience Rochester's cultural side. And with its location in the East End, you're perfectly positioned to grab dinner or drinks before or after the show.

6. Get Wild at the Seneca Park Zoo

Address: 2222 St Paul St, Rochester, NY 14621, USA

Hours: Opens 10 am

Phone: +1 585-336-7200

Animal lovers won't want to miss the Seneca Park Zoo. While it might not be the biggest zoo you've ever visited, it's well-maintained and home to a diverse collection of animals from around the world.

One of the highlights is the "A Step Into Africa" exhibit, where you can see African elephants, lions, and zebras in naturalistic habitats. The zoo also has a strong focus on conservation and education, so you'll come away having learned something new about wildlife and environmental protection.

If you're visiting with kids, be sure to check out the zoo's playground and the tram ride around the park. It's a great way to rest your feet while still seeing the animals.

8. Sip and Savor on the Finger Lakes Wine Trail

While not technically in Rochester, the nearby Finger Lakes wine region is a must-visit for any wine enthusiast. Just a short drive from the city, you'll find yourself in a picturesque landscape of rolling hills, pristine lakes, and world-class wineries.

The Finger Lakes are particularly known for their Rieslings, but you'll find a wide variety of wines to suit every palate. Many wineries offer tours and tastings, allowing you to learn about the winemaking process while enjoying the fruits of their labor.

Even if you're not a big wine drinker, the scenic drive and beautiful lake views make this a worthwhile day trip from Rochester.

9. Get Inspired at the Memorial Art Gallery

Address: 500 University Ave, Rochester, NY 14607, USA

Hours: Opens 11 am

Founded: 1913

Phone: +1 585-276-8900

Director: Sarah Jesse

Art lovers shouldn't miss the Memorial Art Gallery, affectionately known as the MAG. This comprehensive museum houses more than 12,000 works of art spanning 5,000 years of human creativity.

From ancient Egyptian artifacts to contemporary installations, the MAG offers a diverse and engaging collection. The museum also hosts rotating exhibitions, so there's always something new to see.

Don't miss the Centennial Sculpture Park surrounding the museum. It's a beautiful outdoor space featuring works by renowned sculptors and makes for a lovely stroll on a nice day.

Memorial Art Gallery

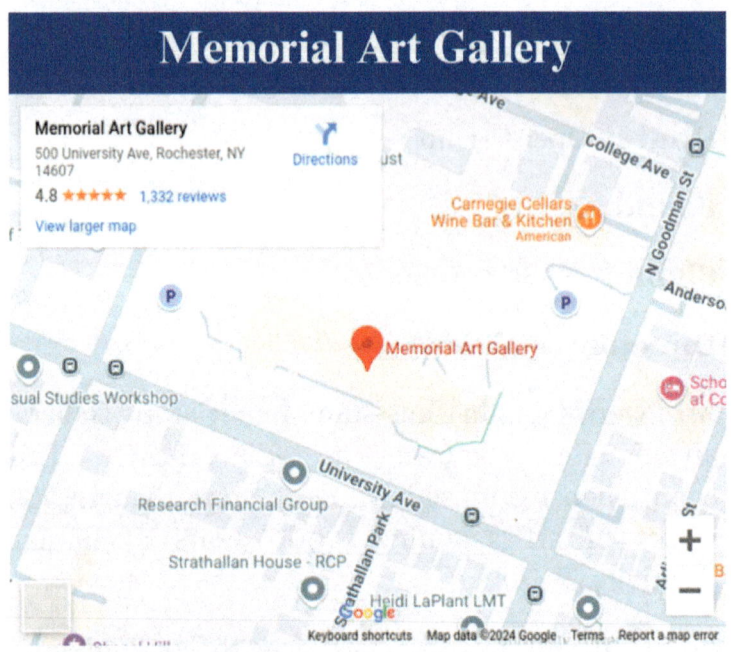

Memorial Art Gallery
500 University Ave, Rochester, NY 14607

★ Directions

4.8 ★★★★★ 1,332 reviews

View larger map

1. Open your device's camera app.
2. Point the camera at the QR code.
3. Ensure the QR code is within the frame and well-lit.
4. Wait for the scanner to recognize and read the code.
5. Tap on the notification or follow the prompt to open the link.
6. Allow access to your location if prompted.
7. View and interact with the map on Google Maps.

10. Take a Cruise on the Erie Canal

The Erie Canal played a crucial role in Rochester's history, and you can experience a bit of that history yourself by taking a cruise along the canal. Sam Patch Erie Canal Tours offers narrated cruises that provide insights into the canal's construction and its impact on the region's development.

As you cruise along the calm waters, you'll pass through locks, under lift bridges, and get a unique perspective on the area's landscape. It's a relaxing way to spend an afternoon and a great opportunity to learn about an important piece of American history.

Bonus: Attend a Rochester Red Wings Game

If you're a baseball fan (or even if you're not), catching a Rochester Red Wings game is a quintessential Rochester experience. The Red Wings are the city's minor league baseball team, and their games at Frontier Field are a beloved summer tradition.

The atmosphere at Frontier Field is fun and family-friendly, with plenty of between-inning entertainment and great ballpark food. Even if you're not a die-hard baseball fan, the relaxed vibe and community spirit make for a enjoyable evening out.

From its rich cultural institutions to its natural beauty and culinary delights, Rochester offers a diverse array of experiences for visitors. Whether you're exploring the city's history, indulging in its food scene, or enjoying its outdoor attractions, you're sure to find something that captures your interest in this vibrant New York city. So come and discover why Rochester is more than just a stopover – it's a destination in its own right.

Family-Friendly Activities in Rochester NY

Hey there, fellow parents and caregivers! If you're planning a trip to Rochester, NY with your kiddos, or if you're a local looking for some fresh ideas to keep the little ones entertained, you've come to the right place. Rochester is a fantastic city for families, with tons of activities that'll keep both kids and adults happy. So, let's dive into some of the best family-friendly spots this city has to offer!

1. The Strong National Museum of Play

First up on our list (and trust me, it's a favorite) is The Strong National Museum of Play. This place is an absolute paradise for kids and, let's be honest, for us big kids at heart too!

Imagine a massive building filled to the brim with interactive exhibits all about... play! Your little ones can explore a mini Wegmans grocery store, climb through a larger-than-life treehouse from the Berenstain Bears books, or try their hand at being a superhero. And for us parents who grew up in the 80s and 90s, there's a whole section dedicated to vintage video games. Talk about a nostalgia trip!

Pro tip: Plan to spend at least half a day here. There's so much to see and do, you'll be glad you set aside the time.

2. Seneca Park Zoo

Next up, we've got the Seneca Park Zoo. It's not the biggest zoo you'll ever visit, but it's got a charm all its own and is perfectly sized for a family outing.

The zoo is home to over 90 species of animals, including crowd-pleasers like elephants, lions, and penguins. One of the coolest parts? The zoo is committed to conservation, so your kids will not only have fun but learn something too. Win-win!

If you've got little ones who tire easily, don't worry. The zoo offers a tram ride that circles the park, giving you a chance to rest those feet while still seeing the animals.

3. Seabreeze Amusement Park

When the weather's nice (because let's face it, Rochester winters can be tough), Seabreeze Amusement Park is the place to be. It's one of the oldest operating amusement parks in the country, but don't let that fool you – it's kept up with the times!

There's a great mix of rides for all ages, from gentle kiddie rides to thrill-seeking roller coasters. And on those hot summer days, the water park section is a lifesaver. Nothing beats watching your kids squeal with delight as they splash down the water slides!

4. Rochester Museum & Science Center

Got some budding scientists or curious minds in your family? The Rochester Museum & Science Center is a must-visit. This place makes learning fun with hands-on exhibits that cover everything from the human body to outer space.

One of the highlights is the Strasenburgh Planetarium, where you can lean back and gaze at the stars. It's a great way to spark those big questions kids love to ask (and sometimes stump us with).

5. Highland Park

Sometimes, the best family activities are the simplest ones. Highland Park is a beautiful green space that's perfect for a family picnic or a game of frisbee.

If you're visiting in May, you're in for a treat. The park hosts the annual Lilac Festival, where you can see (and smell) over 500 varieties of lilacs in bloom. It's a feast for the senses and a great way to teach kids about nature.

Even if you miss the festival, the park has lovely walking trails and playgrounds that are enjoyable year-round.

6. Genesee Country Village & Museum

Want to take a step back in time? The Genesee Country Village & Museum is like a living history book. It's the largest living history museum in New York State, with costumed interpreters who bring the 19th century to life.

Kids can see what school was like in a one-room schoolhouse, watch a blacksmith at work, or even try some old-fashioned games. It's a hands-on way to learn about history that beats any textbook.

7. Ontario Beach Park

When the summer heat hits, there's no better place to cool off than Ontario Beach Park. This beautiful beach on the shores of Lake Ontario is a great spot for building sandcastles, splashing in the water, or just soaking up some sun.

There's also a historic carousel that the kids will love, and plenty of space for a family picnic. Just remember to pack the sunscreen!

8. Memorial Art Gallery

I know what you're thinking – an art gallery with kids? Trust me on this one. The Memorial Art Gallery isn't your typical "don't touch anything" kind of place. They have some great programs designed specifically for families.

Check out their "Family Days" events, where kids can create their own art projects inspired by the gallery's collections. It's a fantastic way to introduce your little ones to the world of art in a fun, approachable way.

9. Wickham Farms

If you're visiting in the fall, Wickham Farms is the place to be. This family-owned farm offers all the classic autumn activities: pumpkin picking, a corn maze, hayrides, you name it.

They also have a pretty awesome jumping pillow (think bouncy castle, but bigger) that's a hit with kids of all ages. And let's not forget the apple cider donuts – they're to die for!

10. Rochester Red Wings Baseball Game

Last but not least, how about taking in a baseball game? The Rochester Red Wings, the city's minor league team, play at Frontier Field, and their games are incredibly family-friendly.

The atmosphere is more relaxed than a major league game, and there are often fun between-inning activities for kids. Plus, the tickets are affordable, making it a great option for families on a budget.

So there you have it, folks! Ten fantastic family-friendly activities in Rochester, NY. Whether you're braving the winter chill or soaking up the summer sun, this city has something for families in every season. Remember, the best family memories often come from the simplest moments, so don't stress too much about planning the perfect itinerary. Just get out there and have fun exploring all that Rochester has to offer!

Shopping in Rochester

Hey there, fellow shoppers! Are you hoping to snag some unique souvenirs? You're in for a treat. Rochester's got a little bit of everything when it comes to shopping - from bustling malls to quaint boutiques and everything in between. So, let's dive into where to shop and what to buy in the Flower City!

Where to Shop

1. Eastview Mall

Address: 7979 Pittsford Victor Rd, Victor, NY 14564, USA

Hours: Opens 10 am

Opened: 1971

Owner: Wilmorite Properties

Phone: +1 585-223-4420

First up on our list is Eastview Mall, and let me tell you, this place is a shopper's paradise. Located in Victor, just a short drive from downtown Rochester, Eastview is the go-to spot for all your favorite brands.

You'll find all the usual suspects here - Macy's, JCPenney, and Von Maur anchor the mall. But what really sets Eastview apart are some of the higher-end stores you won't find at every mall. We're talking Pottery Barn, Apple, and even a Tesla showroom!

Pro tip: If you're shopping with kids (or impatient partners), there's a fantastic play area in the food court. It's a lifesaver when you need just five more minutes to browse.

2. Park Avenue

Address: 31 Rochester Dr, Singapore 138637

Phone: +65 6808 8600

Now, if you're looking for something with a bit more local flavor, head to Park Avenue. This charming street is lined with unique boutiques, cafes, and specialty shops. It's the perfect place to spend a lazy Saturday afternoon, popping in and out of stores.

Some must-visit spots on Park Ave include:

- Parkleigh: A gift shop extraordinaire with everything from gourmet foods to funky home decor.
- Craft Company No. 6: Housed in a converted church, this shop is a treasure trove of handmade crafts and jewelry.
- Dado Boutique: For those looking for stylish, contemporary women's clothing.

3. Village Gate Square

Address: 274 N Goodman St, Rochester, NY 14607, USA

Hours: Opens 9:30 am

Phone: +1 585-442-9061

For a shopping experience with an artistic twist, check out Village Gate Square. This former factory has been transformed into a cool, eclectic mix of shops, restaurants, and art studios.

Highlight stores include:

- Mood Makers Books: A fantastic independent bookstore specializing in African American literature.

- Headz Up Hats: Because who doesn't need a new hat?
- Ritual Clay Company: For beautiful, locally-made ceramics.

4. Public Market

Okay, so the Public Market isn't your typical "shopping" destination, but trust me, you don't want to miss it. Open year-round on Tuesdays, Thursdays, and Saturdays, this market is a feast for the senses.

While it's primarily known for fresh produce, you'll also find flowers, specialty foods, and even some crafts. It's the perfect place to stock up on local goodies or grab some unique edible souvenirs.

4. The Marketplace Mall

Address: 1 Miracle Mile Dr, Rochester, NY 14623, United States

Owner: Wilmorite Properties

Hours: Opens 10 am

Phone: +1 585-424-6220

If you're looking for great deals, The Marketplace Mall is your spot. It's home to a bunch of outlet stores where you can snag name-brand items at discount prices. They've got everything from Nike and Adidas to Gap and Old Navy.

What to Buy

Now that we've covered where to shop, let's talk about what you should be putting in your shopping bags!

1. Wegmans Products

I know, I know. Buying groceries might not be at the top of your vacation shopping list. But hear me out - Wegmans is a Rochester institution, and their store-brand products are seriously good. Pick up some Wegmans Italian Classics pasta sauce or their Organic Blossom honey. Trust me, your taste buds will thank you.

2. Genesee Beer Gear

Even if you're not a beer drinker, Genesee Brewing Company is a huge part of Rochester's history. Swing by their gift shop and pick up a t-shirt, hat, or even a retro metal sign. It's a great way to take a piece of Rochester home with you.

3. Abbott's Frozen Custard Merchandise

Speaking of local institutions, Abbott's Frozen Custard is a Rochester summer staple. While you can't exactly take the custard home in your suitcase, you can grab an Abbott's t-shirt or mug as a sweet reminder of your visit.

4. Local Art

Rochester has a thriving arts scene, and what better souvenir than a piece of local art? Check out the Rochester Contemporary Art Center or one of the many galleries in the Neighborhood of the Arts. You might just find the perfect piece to spruce up your living room!

5. Zweigles' White Hots

Okay, this one's for the foodies. Zweigle's is a local meat company famous for their "white hots" - a unique type of hot dog that's a Rochester specialty. You can pick these up at most local grocery stores. They make for a great (and tasty) souvenir!

6. Rochester-Themed Gear

For straight-up Rochester pride, head to Archimage on Monroe Avenue. They've got a great selection of Rochester-themed t-shirts, mugs, and other knick-knacks. My personal favorite? The "Keep Rochester Weird" bumper sticker!

So there you have it, folks! A whirlwind tour of shopping in Rochester. Whether you're hunting for high-end fashion, unique local goods, or just a fun souvenir, Rochester's got you covered. Happy shopping, and may the sales be ever in your favor!

Nightlife in Rochester

Hey there, night owls and party animals! So, you've found yourself in Rochester, NY, and you're wondering what this city has to offer after the sun goes down. Well, buckle up, because you're in for a treat! Rochester might not be New York City, but don't let that fool you – this mid-sized city knows how to party. From cozy pubs to thumping dance clubs, from live music venues to quirky themed bars, Rochester's got a little something for everyone. Let's dive into the best of Rochester's nightlife!

East End District: The Heart of Rochester Nightlife

First stop on our nocturnal tour is the East End District. This is where the action is, folks!

1. Vertex Night Club

Address: 169 N Chestnut St, Rochester, NY 14604, USA

Hours: Opens 10 pm Thu

Phone: +1 585-232-5498

If you're looking to dance the night away, Vertex is your spot. This multi-level club is the place to see and be seen in Rochester. With state-of-the-art sound and lighting systems, multiple bars, and DJs spinning everything from Top 40 hits to EDM, Vertex is where you go when you want to party hard.

Pro tip: Get there before 11 PM to avoid the long lines. And ladies, Thursday nights are usually Ladies' Night – hello, free drinks!

2. Murphy's Law Irish Pub

Address: 370 East Ave, Rochester, NY 14604, USA

Hours: Opens 11:30 am

Phone: +1 585-232-7115

Need a break from the thumping bass? Head over to Murphy's Law. This Irish pub is the perfect spot for a pint of Guinness and some good craic (that's Irish for fun, by the way). They often have live music, and their outdoor patio is a great place to chill on a warm summer night.

3. Anthology

Address: 336 East Ave, Rochester, NY 14604, United States

Phone: +1 585-484-1964

Music lovers, this one's for you. Anthology is one of Rochester's premier live music venues. They host a wide variety of acts, from up-and-coming local bands to nationally known artists. The sound quality is top-notch, and the atmosphere is always electric.

South Wedge: The Hip and Happening 'Hood

If you're looking for something a little more laid-back and eclectic, head to the South Wedge neighborhood.

4. Lux Lounge

Address: 666 South Ave, Rochester, NY 14620, USA

Hours: Opens 4 pm

Lux is... well, Lux is an experience. This dive bar is known for its quirky decor (think random dolls and bizarre artwork), strong drinks, and friendly crowd. It's the kind of place where you can strike up a conversation with a stranger and end up making a new best friend.

5. Tap and Mallet

Address: 381 Gregory St, Rochester, NY 14620, United States

Phone: +1 585-473-0503

Calling all beer snobs! I mean, craft beer enthusiasts. Tap and Mallet is your heaven. With over 30 beers on tap and an ever-changing selection, you're sure to find your new favorite brew here. The laid-back atmosphere and knowledgeable staff make this a great spot to start your night.

Park Ave: Classy Nightlife

For a slightly more upscale experience, Park Ave is where it's at.

6. Magpie Irish Pub

Address: 653 Park Ave, Rochester, NY 14607, USA

Hours: Opens 1 pm

Phone: +1 585-271-4150

Don't let the word "pub" fool you – Magpie is classy. With its dark wood interior and extensive whiskey selection, it's the perfect spot for a sophisticated night out. They also have a great outdoor seating area for those perfect Rochester summer nights.

7. Dragonfly Tavern

Address: 725 Park Ave, Rochester, NY 14607, United States

Hours: Opens 4 pm

Phone: +1 585-563-6333

If craft cocktails are your thing, you've got to check out Dragonfly Tavern. Their mixologists (yeah, that's a thing) create some of the most inventive and delicious drinks in the city. The speakeasy vibe adds to the experience – you'll feel like you've stepped back in time to the Roaring Twenties.

Unique Nightlife Experiences

Now, if you're looking for something a little different, Rochester's got you covered there too.

8. Radio Social

Address: 20 Carlson Rd, Rochester, NY 14610, USA

Hours: Opens 4:30 pm

Phone: +1 585-244-1484

Bowling alley meets nightclub? Yes, please! Radio Social is a massive space that includes bowling lanes, ping pong tables, arcade games, and a restaurant and bar. It's the perfect spot for a group outing or a unique date night.

9. The Spirit Room

Address: 139 State St, Rochester, NY 14614, USA

Hours: Opens 5 pm

Phone: +1 585-705-9937

For a truly one-of-a-kind experience, check out The Spirit Room. This occult-themed cocktail bar is decked out in Victorian-era decor and serves up drinks with names like "Hellfire" and "Séance." They often have tarot card readers and other spooky entertainment. It's weird, it's wonderful, and it's totally Rochester.

10. Comedy at Comedy @ the Carlson

Address: 50 Carlson Rd, Rochester, NY 14610, USA

Phone: +1 585-426-6339

Need a good laugh? Comedy @ the Carlson hosts both local comedians and national acts. It's a great way to start your night with some laughs before hitting the bars.

Late Night Munchies

All that partying is bound to work up an appetite. For late-night eats, check out:

- Dogtown: Open until 1 AM on weekends, their gourmet hot dogs are the perfect post-bar snack.
- Mark's Texas Hots: A Rochester institution, open 24/7. Their garbage plates are legendary (and yes, that's really what they're called).

Getting Around

Quick note on transportation: while Rochester does have public buses, they don't run very late. Your best bet for getting around at night is going to be ride-sharing services like Uber or Lyft. And of course, if you're drinking, always plan for a safe ride home!

So there you have it, folks – your guide to painting the town red in Rochester! Whether you're looking to dance until dawn, enjoy some live music, or just have a few quiet drinks with friends, Rochester's nightlife has got you covered. Now get out there and experience the best that Rochester after dark has to offer. Just don't blame me for your hangover tomorrow morning!

Exciting Day Trips from Rochester, New York: Your Ultimate Guide

Let's face it, as much as we love Rochester, sometimes we all need a little change of scenery. The good news? The Flower City is perfectly positioned for some fantastic day trips. Whether you're a nature enthusiast, a history buff, or just looking for a new adventure, there's something for everyone within a few hours' drive. So, gas up the car, pack some snacks, and let's hit the road!

1. Niagara Falls: A Natural Wonder Just a Stone's Throw Away

Distance from Rochester: About 90 miles (145 km)

Estimated drive time: 1.5 to 2 hours

Okay, let's start with the obvious. Niagara Falls is practically in our backyard, and it never gets old. Trust me, I've been there dozens of times, and I still get goosebumps when I hear the roar of the falls.

What to do:

- Take a ride on the Maid of the Mist. Yes, you'll get wet. No, you won't regret it.
- Walk the Cave of the Winds. It's like nature's own shower system.

- Enjoy the view from the observation tower at Prospect Point.
- Cross the Rainbow Bridge into Canada for a different perspective (don't forget your passport!).

Pro tip: Go early to beat the crowds, especially in summer. And bring a change of clothes – you'll thank me later.

2. Letchworth State Park: The "Grand Canyon of the East"

Distance from Rochester: About 40 miles (64 km)

Estimated drive time: 45 minutes to 1 hour

If you haven't been to Letchworth yet, what are you waiting for? This place is a nature lover's paradise, especially in fall when the foliage is on fire (not literally, of course).

What to do:

- Hike the Gorge Trail for breathtaking views of the waterfalls.
- Take a hot air balloon ride for a bird's eye view of the park (book in advance!).
- Visit the William Pryor Letchworth Museum to learn about the park's history.

- Go white water rafting if you're feeling adventurous.

Personal experience: Last autumn, I packed a picnic and spent the whole day exploring the trails. The colors were unreal, and I got some of the best photos I've ever taken. Just remember to wear sturdy shoes – some of those trails can be slippery!

3. Finger Lakes Wine Country: Sip and Savor

Distance from Rochester: Varies, but most wineries are within 50-90 miles (80-145 km)

Estimated drive time: 1 to 2 hours, depending on which lake you choose

Wine lovers, rejoice! We're lucky enough to have one of the best wine regions in the country right in our backyard. The Finger Lakes area is dotted with over 100 wineries, and each one has its own unique charm.

What to do:

- Take a wine tour (please drink responsibly and consider a designated driver or tour service).
- Visit Dr. Konstantin Frank Winery, one of the oldest in the region.

- Stop by the New York Kitchen in Canandaigua for a culinary class.
- Enjoy the scenery – those lake views are something else!

Insider tip: Don't sleep on the Rieslings. The Finger Lakes region is known for them, and they're seriously good. Even if you think you don't like sweet wines, give them a try. You might be surprised!

4. Corning Museum of Glass: A Transparent Wonder

Distance from Rochester: About 100 miles (160 km)

Estimated drive time: 2 hours

Glass might not sound exciting, but trust me, this place is cool. It's a perfect mix of art, science, and history, and you can even make your own glass souvenir!

What to do:

- Watch live glassblowing demonstrations (it's mesmerizing, I promise).
- Try your hand at making your own glass in a short workshop.

- Explore the contemporary art gallery – some of those pieces will blow your mind.
- Check out the optical fiber exhibit to see how modern communication works.

5. Watkins Glen State Park: A Gorge-ous Getaway

Distance from Rochester: About 90 miles (145 km)

Estimated drive time: 1.5 to 2 hours

If you're into Instagram-worthy landscapes, Watkins Glen is your spot. The gorge trail feels like something out of a fantasy novel, with 19 waterfalls along its 2-mile path.

What to do:

- Hike the Gorge Trail (but be prepared for lots of steps).
- Take a dip in the Olympic-sized pool at the park entrance.
- Visit in different seasons – it's stunning year-round.
- Combine it with a trip to the Finger Lakes wineries for a full day out.

Word of caution: The trails can get slippery, especially after rain. Wear good shoes and take it slow. The views are worth savoring anyway!

6. 1000 Islands: A Water Lover's Paradise

Distance from Rochester: About 150 miles (240 km)

Estimated drive time: 2.5 to 3 hours

Okay, this one's pushing the limits of a "day trip," but it's so worth it. The 1000 Islands region is a gorgeous maze of waterways and tiny islands, with enough activities to fill a whole weekend.

What to do:

- Take a boat tour to see Boldt Castle (it's like a fairy tale come to life).
- Go kayaking or paddleboarding between the islands.
- Visit the Antique Boat Museum in Clayton.
- Enjoy fresh fish at one of the many waterfront restaurants.

Pro tip: If you can, stay overnight. The sunsets over the St. Lawrence River are something special, and you'll have more time to explore without feeling rushed.

7. Syracuse: Urban Adventure Just Down the Thruway

Distance from Rochester: About 90 miles (145 km)

Estimated drive time: 1.5 hours

Sometimes you want a change of pace without straying too far from city life. Syracuse fits the bill perfectly, offering a mix of history, culture, and fun.

What to do:

- Explore the Erie Canal Museum to learn about the waterway that shaped New York.
- Shop till you drop at Destiny USA, one of the largest malls in the country.
- Catch a game at the Carrier Dome if you're a sports fan.
- Visit the Everson Museum of Art for a dose of culture.

There you have it – a whirlwind tour of some of the best day trips from Rochester. Whether you're looking to commune with nature, sip some wine, learn something new, or just escape the daily grind, there's an adventure waiting for you just a short drive away.

Remember, half the fun of a day trip is the journey itself. Don't be afraid to take the scenic route, stop at that quirky roadside attraction, or pull over for a spontaneous picnic. Some of my best memories are from those unplanned moments.

So, what are you waiting for? Pick a destination, grab your keys, and go explore. Rochester is great, but there's a whole world out there just waiting to be discovered. Happy travels!

Chapter Six: Photography Guide

Photography Tips for Rochester Travelers

Hey there, shutterbug! So you're ready to capture the essence of Rochester through your lens, huh? Well, you're in for a treat. This city is a photographer's playground, with its mix of urban charm, natural beauty, and ever-changing seasons. But before you start snapping away like a tourist on ten espressos, let's chat about some tips to elevate your photos from "meh" to "wow!"

Now, I'm not going to tell you where to point your camera – that's half the fun of exploring Rochester yourself. Instead, I'm going to arm you with some general photography wisdom that'll serve you well whether you're shooting our stunning waterfalls or trying to capture the perfect "cheese pull" from a slice of Rochester pizza. (Spoiler alert: it's harder than it looks!)

So, grab your camera, and let's dive into some tips that'll make your Instagram followers green with envy:

1. **Chase the light, not the landmarks**: Rochester's got some killer "golden hours" – that magical time just after sunrise or before sunset. The light is soft, warm, and makes everything look like it's been touched by King Midas. Set that alarm clock early or delay your dinner plans – your photos will thank you.

2. **Embrace the weather**: Look, Rochester isn't exactly known for its year-round sunshine. But that's no reason to keep your camera tucked away. Rainy days? Perfect for moody street shots. Snowy days? Hello, winter wonderland! Every weather condition is an opportunity for unique shots.

3. **Get low, get high**: Change your perspective! Crouch down low or find a high vantage point. You'll be amazed how different familiar scenes can look when you're not shooting at eye level. Just, you know, be careful if you're climbing things. We want great photos, not hospital visits.

4. **Rule of thirds is your friend**: Imagine your frame divided into a 3x3 grid. Try placing your main subject along these lines

or at their intersections. It's a simple trick that can dramatically improve your composition. Most smartphone cameras even have a grid option – use it!

5. **Details, details, details**: Sure, sweeping vistas are great, but don't forget to zoom in on the little things. The texture of bark in our parks, the intricate architecture on our historical buildings, the steam rising from a cup of local coffee – these details tell Rochester's story too.

6. **Patience is a virtue**: Sometimes the perfect shot means waiting. For the right light, for people to move out of (or into) your frame, for that quintessential Rochester moment. Slow down, observe, and be ready.

7. **Talk to locals**: Rochesterians are a friendly bunch, and they know this city better than any guidebook. Strike up a conversation, and you might just get tipped off to some hidden photographic gems.

8. **Don't forget to put the camera down**: I know, I know, this sounds counterintuitive in a photography tip list. But sometimes, the best way to capture the essence of Rochester is to experience it fully, without a lens between you and the moment. Your memory can be the best photograph of all.

Remember, the best camera is the one you have with you, whether that's a fancy DSLR or your smartphone. Rochester's beauty isn't picky – it shines through regardless of your gear. So get out there, have fun, and show the world Rochester through your eyes. Who knows? You might just capture a shot that makes even us locals see our city in a new light!

Rochester's Most Photogenic Locations

Picture this: you're in Rochester, camera in hand, itching to capture some Instagram-worthy shots. Where do you go? Well, buckle up, my photography-loving friend, because I'm about to take you on a whirlwind tour of Rochester's most camera-friendly spots!

First stop: High Falls. Trust me, this isn't just some little trickle. We're talking about a 96-foot waterfall right in the heart of downtown. It's like Mother Nature decided to plonk a slice of wilderness in the middle of the city. Pro tip: catch it at sunset for some truly epic shots.

Next up, let's take a stroll through Highland Park. In spring, this place explodes with color during the Lilac Festival. It's like someone spilled a giant bottle of purple paint all over the park. Even if you miss the lilacs, the arboretum is a year-round feast for the eyes.

Now, how about some architectural eye candy? The George Eastman Museum is a photographer's dream. The mansion itself is gorgeous, but the gardens? Oh boy. They're so pretty, your camera might just start taking pictures on its own out of sheer excitement.

For a taste of Rochester's artsy side, head to the Neighborhood of the Arts (NOTA). The Wall\Therapy murals scattered throughout this area are like a free, open-air art gallery. Plus, you get to look cool and cultured as you snap away.

Let's not forget about the Rochester Public Market. It's a riot of colors, textures, and characters. From fresh produce to quirky vendors, there's a photo op around every corner. Just try not to drool on your camera as you shoot all the delicious-looking food.

For a bit of romance (or just a darn good view), make your way to Cobbs Hill Park at sunset. The city skyline from up there? *Chef's kiss* It's the kind of view that makes you want to write poetry... or at least a really long Instagram caption.

And here's one for the history buffs: Mount Hope Cemetery. Now, I know what you're thinking. A cemetery? Really? But hear me out. This place is stunning, especially in fall when the trees put on a show that'd make Broadway jealous. Plus, you might spot the graves of some famous folks like Susan B. Anthony and Frederick Douglass.

Last but not least, let's head out of the city a bit to Letchworth State Park. They call it the "Grand Canyon of the East," and let me tell you, it lives up to the hype. Waterfalls, gorges, forests - this place is like nature's greatest hits album.

So there you have it, folks! Rochester's most photogenic spots, served up with a side of local flavor. Remember, the best camera is the one you have with you, so don't stress if you're just working with a smartphone. Rochester's beauty shines through no matter what. Now get out there and start shooting - those likes aren't going to earn themselves!

Chapter Seven: A Sound Track for Your Journey

Music to Enjoy During a Rochester Vacation

You're cruising down East Avenue, the sun's setting, painting the sky in hues of orange and pink, and you've got the perfect song playing. Suddenly, your Rochester vacation hits a whole new level of awesome. That's the magic of music, folks!

Music isn't just background noise; it's like the secret sauce that can turn a good trip into an unforgettable adventure. It has this uncanny ability to reduce stress, boost your mood, and even make time seem to slow down (in a good way). Plus, the right tunes can really help you soak in the local vibes and create memories that'll stick with you long after you've left the Flower City.

So, what should be on your Rochester vacation playlist? Well, buckle up, because I'm about to drop some suggestions that'll have you bobbing your head all the way from the Strong Museum to the shores of Lake Ontario:

1. "Kodachrome" by Paul Simon - Because, hello, Kodak was born here!

2. "Flower City" by Giant Panda Guerilla Dub Squad - A local band's ode to Rochester

3. "Genesee" by The Demos - Nothing like a song about our river to set the mood

4. "Rochester" by Vampire Weekend - They're not from here, but we'll take the shoutout

5. "Don't You (Forget About Me)" by Simple Minds - A nod to all the unforgettable memories you'll make

6. "Walking in Memphis" by Marc Cohn - He's a Rochester native!

7. "Summertime" by DJ Jazzy Jeff & The Fresh Prince - Perfect for those sunny days by the lake

8. "Lilac Wine" by Jeff Buckley - A subtle nod to our famous Lilac Festival

9. "Higher and Higher" by Jackie Wilson - Because your spirits will be soaring in Rochester

10. "Good Old Days" by Macklemore & Kesha - For when you're feeling nostalgic at the Strong Museum

And hey, don't forget to sprinkle in some local flavors! Check out Rochester-born jazz legend Chuck Mangione, or indie rockers Joywave. Or how about some Danielle Ponder for some soulful vibes?

This is just a starting point. The best playlist is one that makes YOU feel good. So whether you're into classical, hip-hop, country, or anything in between, make sure your Rochester soundtrack is as unique as your trip. Now, hit play and let the good times roll!

Movies for Relaxation in Rochester

You've just spent the day trekking through Highland Park, stuffing your face with Garbage Plates, and snapping a million photos at High Falls. Your feet are aching, your stomach's full, and your brain's buzzing with all the Rochester awesomeness you've soaked up. Now what? It's movie time, my friend!

There's something magical about curling up with a good flick after a day of exploration. It's like hitting the reset button on your brain. Movies have this sneaky way of transporting you to another world while letting your body catch a break. They're the perfect way to process all the cool stuff you've seen and done, without, you know, actually having to move.

Plus, watching a movie set in or related to Rochester? That's like extending your sightseeing from the comfort of your hotel bed. It's armchair tourism at its finest! You might spot places you've just visited or learn some quirky fact about the city that'll make you the star of tomorrow's conversations.

So, without further ado, here's a list of movies perfect for your Rochester relaxation session:

1. "The Wizard of Oz" (1939) - Okay, it's not set in Rochester, but parts of it were filmed at Kodak! Plus, it's the ultimate comfort movie.

2. "Spider-Man: Homecoming" (2017) - Some scenes were shot in Rochester. Spot any familiar locations?

3. "The Alphabet Killer" (2008) - A thriller based on the unsolved Alphabet murders in Rochester. Maybe not relaxing, but definitely local!

4. "The Incredibly True Adventure of Two Girls in Love" (1995) - This charming indie film was shot in and around Rochester.

5. "Anomalisa" (2015) - An animated film co-directed by Rochester native Charlie Kaufman. It's quirky, it's thought-provoking, it's perfect for unwinding.

6. "The Lodger" (1944) - A classic thriller with scenes shot at the George Eastman House. Movie history and local landmarks in one package!

7. "Lady in White" (1988) - A supernatural thriller filmed in Wayne County, just east of Rochester. Local scenery with a side of spookiness!

8. "The Natural" (1984) - While set in New York City, much of it was filmed in Buffalo, giving you a taste of Western New York.

9. "Planes, Trains and Automobiles" (1987) - Not Rochester-specific, but it captures the spirit of travel mishaps. Perfect for laughing off any vacation hiccups!

10. "It's a Wonderful Life" (1946) - The ultimate feel-good movie. Fun fact: the city of Bedford Falls was partially inspired by Seneca Falls, NY, not far from Rochester.

The best movie is one that helps you relax. So if none of these float your boat, no worries! Pop on your personal favorite, order some local snacks (Zweigles hot dogs, anyone?), and let the silver screen work its magic. After all, the point is to recharge for another day of Rochester adventures. Lights, camera, relaxation!

Chapter Eight: Itinerary

Rochester 3-Day Itinerary

Hey there, Rochester explorer! Planning a quick weekend getaway or a full week of adventure in the Flower City, I've got you covered. This itinerary is packed with the best Rochester has to offer, from cultural attractions to outdoor adventures, and of course, plenty of great food and drink. Let's dive in!

Day 1: City Highlights

Morning:

- Start your day at the Rochester Public Market. Grab breakfast at one of the market cafes and explore the vibrant stalls.
- Head to the George Eastman Museum. Explore the stunning mansion and learn about the history of photography.

Afternoon:

- Lunch at the Dinosaur Bar-B-Que for some killer ribs and blues music.
- Visit the Strong National Museum of Play. Trust me, it's not just for kids!

Evening:

- Dinner at Good Luck Restaurant for farm-to-table cuisine and craft cocktails.
- Catch a show at Geva Theatre or live music at Anthology.

Day 2: Nature and Science

Morning:

- Breakfast at Highland Park Diner, then explore Highland Park itself. If it's May, you might catch the Lilac Festival!
- Visit the Rochester Museum & Science Center and catch a show at the Strasenburgh Planetarium.

Afternoon:

- Grab lunch at Abbott's Frozen Custard (a local institution) near Lake Ontario.

- Spend the afternoon at Ontario Beach Park. Take a stroll on the pier and ride the historic Dentzel Carousel.

Evening:

- Dinner at The Cub Room in the South Wedge neighborhood.
- Bar hopping in the South Wedge. Don't miss Lux Lounge and Tap & Mallet.

Day 3: Art and Culture

Morning:

- Breakfast at Jines Restaurant on Park Avenue.
- Explore the Memorial Art Gallery and its sculpture garden.

Afternoon:

- Lunch at Magnolia's Deli & Cafe.
- Take a stroll down the pedestrian bridge for a view of High Falls, then visit the High Falls Interpretive Center.

Evening:

- Dinner at REDD, one of Rochester's top fine dining restaurants.
- End your trip with bowling and drinks at Radio Social.

Rochester One-Week Itinerary

For a week-long stay, start with the 3-day itinerary above, then add these activities:

Day 4: Family Fun

Morning:

- Breakfast at Village Bakery & Cafe.
- Spend the morning at the Seneca Park Zoo.

Afternoon:

- Lunch at Bill Gray's, home of the famous "World's Greatest Cheeseburger".
- Afternoon at Seabreeze Amusement Park (seasonal) or indoor rock climbing at RocVentures.

Evening:

- Dinner at Dinosaur Bar-B-Que (if you missed it earlier).
- Catch a Rochester Red Wings baseball game at Frontier Field (seasonal).

Day 5: Historical Rochester

Morning:

- Breakfast at Flour City Diner.
- Visit the Susan B. Anthony House and Museum.

Afternoon:

- Lunch at Swan Market for authentic German fare.
- Explore Genesee Country Village & Museum, a 19th-century living history museum.

Evening:

- Dinner at Rooney's Restaurant, housed in a beautiful old mansion.
- Ghost tour with Haunted History Ghost Walk (seasonal).

Day 6: Outdoor Adventure

Morning:

- Grab breakfast to go from Boxcar Donuts and head to Letchworth State Park, "The Grand Canyon of the East".
- Hike the gorge trails and see the magnificent waterfalls.

Afternoon:

- Picnic lunch in the park.
- Continue exploring Letchworth or head back to Rochester for some shopping at Eastview Mall or the boutiques on Park Avenue.

Evening:

- Dinner at Next Door by Wegmans, experiencing the best of Rochester's famous grocery chain.
- Enjoy craft cocktails at The Spirit Room.

Day 7: Finger Lakes Day Trip

Morning:

- Early breakfast at James Brown's Place.
- Drive to the Finger Lakes region (about an hour from Rochester).

- Visit a few wineries on Seneca Lake or Keuka Lake.

Afternoon:

- Lunch with a view at Belhurst Castle in Geneva.
- Continue wine tasting or visit the Corning Museum of Glass.

Evening:

- Head back to Rochester for a farewell dinner at Tournedos Steakhouse.
- Cap off your trip with drinks at the revolving restaurant at the Top of the Plaza for panoramic city views.

These itineraries are just suggestions - feel free to mix and match based on your interests, the weather, and any special events happening during your visit. Rochester has so much to offer, you might just find yourself planning your next trip before this one is over!

"The journey of a thousand miles begins with a single step." – Lao Tzu

Chapter Nine: Farewell, Rochester

Until We Meet Again

As the sun sets over the Genesee River, casting a golden glow on the city skyline, it's hard not to feel a twinge of sadness. Rochester, with its tree-lined streets, vibrant culture, and warm-hearted people, has a way of capturing the hearts of those who visit. It's not goodbye, but rather, "until we meet again."

Rochester surprises at every turn. What might seem like just another mid-sized city in upstate New York reveals itself to be a weave of experiences, each thread weaving a story of history, innovation, and community spirit. From the moment visitors arrive, they're embraced by the city's unique charm and welcoming atmosphere.

The streets of Rochester whisper tales of the past. In the Susan B. Anthony neighborhood, one can almost hear the echoes of determined footsteps marching towards equality. The George Eastman Museum stands as a testament to the city's role in shaping modern photography, its halls filled with images that capture moments frozen in time.

But Rochester isn't content to live in the past. It pulses with a vibrant energy, evident in the bustling Public Market on a Saturday morning. Here, the aroma of fresh produce mingles with the scent of artisanal breads and locally roasted coffee. The chatter of vendors and shoppers creates a symphony of community, a reminder that in Rochester, strangers quickly become friends.

The city's palate is as diverse as its people. From the infamous "garbage plate" that has become a cultural icon, to the delicate flavors of farm-to-table restaurants, Rochester's culinary scene is a journey in itself. And let's not forget the sweet taste of Abbott's frozen custard on a warm summer evening - a flavor that lingers in memory long after the last spoonful is gone.

Nature embraces the city in a gentle hug. The lilacs in Highland Park burst into a riot of color and fragrance each spring, painting the landscape in hues of purple and white. The thundering waters of High Falls remind us of nature's power, even in the heart of the city. And just a short drive away, the

Finger Lakes beckon with their serene beauty and world-class wineries.

As night falls, Rochester comes alive in a different way. The sound of laughter drifts from cozy pubs in the South Wedge. Music spills out of venues like Anthology, where both local talents and national acts take the stage. In the East End, the clinking of glasses and the hum of conversation create a backdrop for memories in the making.

What truly sets Rochester apart, though, is its people. Their friendliness isn't just a facade for tourists; it's a genuine warmth that envelops visitors, making them feel like longtime residents. It's the barista who remembers your order, the shopkeeper who shares local tips, the stranger who offers directions with a smile. This spirit of community is Rochester's true magic.

As travelers prepare to leave, they often find themselves already planning their return. There's always more to explore - a festival missed, a trail not yet hiked, a museum exhibit to see. Rochester has a way of leaving a piece of itself with those who visit, while keeping a piece of them in return.

So as bags are packed and final photos are snapped, it's not with heavy hearts that travelers bid farewell to Rochester. Instead, it's with gratitude for the experiences shared, the memories made, and the knowledge that this remarkable city will be here, ever-evolving yet ever-welcoming, when they return.

Farewell, Flower City, but only for now. Keep blooming, keep growing, keep surprising. Your story isn't just written in history books, but in the hearts of all who visit. Until we meet again, Rochester - stay extraordinary.

Chapter Ten: Reflective Journal

Capturing Memories

As you look back on your time in Rochester, take a moment to reflect on your experiences. These questions are designed to help you delve deeper into your memories, emotions, and personal growth during your visit. Feel free to write as much or as little as you'd like for each prompt.

1. **First Impressions**: What was your initial reaction when you arrived in Rochester? How did this change over the course of your visit?

_____

_____

_____

_____

_____

_____

_____

_____

_____

_____

_____

_____

_____

_____

_____

_____

_____

_____

_____

_____

2. **Unexpected Discoveries**: What was the most surprising thing you learned or experienced in Rochester? How did this surprise challenge your preconceptions about the city?

_____

_____

_____

_____

_____

_____

_____

_____

_____

_____

_____

_____

_____

_____

_____

_____

_____

_____

_____

3. **Sensory Memories**: Close your eyes and think about Rochester. What sights, sounds, smells, tastes, or textures come to mind? Which of these sensory experiences was most impactful for you and why?

_____

_____

_____

_____

_____

_____

_____

_____

_____

_____

_____

_____

_____

_____

_____

_____

_____

_____

_____

4. **Cultural Insights**: How did your visit to Rochester broaden your understanding of the city's history or culture? Was there a particular museum, landmark, or event that stood out in this regard?

_____

_____

_____

_____

_____

_____

_____

_____

_____

_____

_____

_____

_____

_____

_____

_____

_____

_____

_____

5. **Personal Growth**: In what ways do you feel you've grown or changed as a result of your experiences in Rochester? Did you try anything new or step out of your comfort zone?

_____

_____

_____

_____

_____

_____

_____

_____

_____

_____

_____

_____

_____

_____

_____

_____

_____

_____

_____

_____

6. **Local Connections**: Describe a meaningful interaction you had with a local resident. What did this encounter teach you about the people of Rochester or about human connection in general?

_____

_____

_____

_____

_____

_____

_____

_____

_____

_____

_____

_____

_____

_____

_____

_____

_____

_____

_____

_____

7. **Natural Beauty**: How did Rochester's natural surroundings impact your visit? Was there a park, waterfall, or outdoor space that left a lasting impression on you?

_____

_____

_____

_____

_____

_____

_____

_____

_____

_____

_____

_____

_____

_____

_____

_____

_____

_____

_____

_____

_____

8. **Culinary Journey**: What was your most memorable food experience in Rochester? How did it reflect the local culture or history?

_____

_____

_____

_____

_____

_____

_____

_____

_____

_____

_____

_____

_____

_____

_____

_____

_____

_____

_____

_____

9. **Emotional Resonance**: Was there a moment during your visit when you felt a strong emotional response (joy, awe, nostalgia, etc.)? Describe this moment and reflect on why it affected you so deeply.

_____

_____

_____

_____

_____

_____

_____

_____

_____

_____

_____

_____

_____

_____

_____

_____

_____

_____

_____

_____

10. **Lasting Impact**: As you leave Rochester, what will you take with you (metaphorically speaking)? How might your experiences in the city influence your future travels or daily life?

_____

_____

_____

_____

_____

_____

_____

_____

_____

_____

_____

_____

_____

_____

_____

_____

_____

_____

Bonus Reflection: If you were to return to Rochester, what would you do differently? What would you make sure to experience again?

_____

_____

_____

_____

_____

_____

_____

_____

_____

_____

_____

_____

_____

_____

_____

_____

_____

_____

_____

_____

_____

_____

_____

_____

Printed in Great Britain
by Amazon

63328857R00080